*"There is Freedom of speech,*

*but*

*I can't guarantee you freedom after speech."*

*- Idi Amin Dada*

# Introduction

This book has been a journey and an incredible blessing in my life. I'm so grateful to be able to share it with whoever this might reach!

This book to me has been a bet that I'm making on the nature of this world. I was brought up in a world of fear. The people in my life were extremely scared of the truth and would use elaborate lies to protect each other from the harshness of reality.

My long journey into the bowels of honesty has been one of incredible contraction and uncomfortable to say the least. The quote from Idi Amin on page three serves as a poignant reminder to me of how far one can stray when fear of the truth takes hold.

I feel lucky and blessed to be where I am today. Honesty has transformed my life and the world around me.

While I don't always believe in God, I find that part of me does believe and part of my journey into honesty has been allowing for me to be a contradiction.

This book is riddled with contradictions, and I travel through the pains and fears of allowing for there to be no answer.

Whether I believe in God or not is one question, but I think that I'm starting to be a believer in a higher power, the power of honesty. The power of not running away. The power of sitting and the power of walking slowly.

I hope this book lands well in you and that this is a pleasant experience for at least part of you.

I'd like to end this Introduction with a prayer.

*Dear God,*

*I'm putting this book out there into the world. I'm trusting something, blindfolding my mind and allowing my voice to come out less filtered.*

*I'm so scared that people won't understand this book and judge me for sounding so confused.*

*You know my heart God and know how imperfect I am.*

*You also know how valuable I think imperfection is.*

*You also know that I'm really fucking trying here.*

*God,*

*Whatever happens with this book, if it's not read or twisted or my own fears come in and I start to twist my own words, not understanding myself and doubting my honesty.*

*Please God, cherish this moment right here and now at this coffee shop where my heart is pure, clear and thick.*

*Let's lock this moment and trust that this is all meant to be and that we are both following the trail of honesty.*

*Thank you, God, for an incredible journey and I look forward to getting lost with you again!*

# *Honest Heated Prayers*

An Agnostic Prayerbook

By Abie Cohen

# Table of Contents

# Becoming Man

He told me that I looked old.

He found the only crease on my face and stretched it for a second.

I remember what my father's hand smelled like as a child.

I had never smelled anything like that and would climb into the recliner as he slept with my face in his hands.

His hands had cracks in them, and he would wake as I opened an old wound.

My father used lotion all the time.

I never use lotion.

My hands are soft, oh so soft.

My hands don't smell weird.

My skin is immaculate, and I don't sleep on recliners.

What is a man?

What am I?

Why am I so clean?

Clean for a man seems like the dirtiest thing.

Like I've cheated my way into manhood.

There was a story about a blind man who lived right off H'lavene square in Bratislava.

People would line up at his window as he handed out the leftovers he had picked up from the bakery.

The children would come around for doubles, the adults would only take one and the old men would give half of it to a child as they left.

I'm so ashamed of who I am in comparison to the men of past.

*God, the hairs on my arms are a mistake.*

*Theres noting man about me.*

*God, where have all the men gone?*

*Did you take them with you and leave all of us pretties?*

*God, I need to look into steady eyes that could carry the weight of death.*

*God, I need to slow down like my grandfather.*

*I need to go so slow that I could walk in completion.*

*God, I read through your whole book and didn't find a definition for man.*

*Can one know what man is or can you only become?*

I remember once feeling man coursing through my veins.

I had no thoughts in my mind.

It was clear and empty.

I didn't want anything.

I didn't need to be anywhere.

My feet were heavy, and my eyes shone.

Colors stacked up beautifully into piles of black and white and my top lip rested on my bottom one.

My Rabbi would make fun of my brightly colored dorm room blanket.

He would wake me up with a new joke every day.

His not man was different than mine.

His not man was boredom while mine was anger.

My senses were sharpened by anger.

I could hear an insult from twenty years away as if it was said right next to me.

My muscles were wound so tight that they turned into a thick coat.

I clunked around with uneven steps.

I wanted answers.

I wanted truths.

I wanted a why for their I knows.

I didn't have questions.

I didn't look only forward or back.

I stood there bewildered with little reason for my temper.

*God, I miss my then.*

*I was so beautiful.*

*So pure.*

*So full of passion.*

*So hungry for your world.*

*I didn't know weakness.*

*I didn't know what no backbone does to the soul.*

*I didn't know that nowhere was somewhere too but with bad neighbors.*

*God, was my Rabbi right?*

*Should I have fit in with the rest of them?*

*Should I have covered my sheets with shoe polish?*

*God, I feel as though I'm living in sin.*

*My soul doesn't fit in my body.*

*I'm rewarded for something that I'm not.*

*God, men are made in the dark and women in the light.*

*We have no dark nowadays and our light is artificial.*

*Will I be too cruel to myself if I force myself into the dark.*

*Can one create darkness or will I become an artificial man.*

*I need to travel far from myself.*

*I need to crawl into the cave where my demons live and let them tear me apart.*

*I can't live on like this.*

*I can't create children with clean hands.*

*It's not fair to them and I wouldn't allow myself to be trusted when my gaze dips.*

*God, why is it that the steadiest minds have the wobbliest hands.*

*God, it's all backwards here.*

*I can't listen to what people say.*

*I have to go find my anger where I left him and learn how to take the bread given to me by all that is blind.*

*God, I love you with all my heart, but I have to go away even from you for a bit and hate it all.*

*God, we might not meet for a while but just know that no matter where I go, you are on the other side of my down under.*

*I'm going to miss all this cleanliness so much.*

*I can't believe I'm walking away from what I want.*

*I can't believe I'm dropping it all...*

# Neglected

I want to be an anchor.

I want to sing and fly and live and die.

I want to climb and fall and roll and crumble.

I want to stretch and fold and lift and tumble.

I want to eat and speak and gasp and cough.

I want the trip and bend and twist.

I want to be humbled.

I want to be taught a lesson.

For a voice to scream out and acknowledge my existence.

*I feel neglected by you God.*

*If it was just abuse, I'd take it.*

*If it was just abuse, then I'd wear the abuse on my skin with pride.*

*If it was abuse, I would back you up to all your deniers.*

*I'd tell them that they don't know the full story.*

*That they can't see how you are with me.*

*That I know you, like really know you and that you are just misunderstood.*

*But it's not abuse.*

*I don't exist do I.*

*I could scream and shout and stomp my feet loudly and you wouldn't budge.*

*I could slam my feet on your table, but nothing would move.*

*Even if I break the darn thing, something else will come and take its place.*

*My contribution to the now broken table would be explained away.*

*I would be explained away.*

*I am living a meaningless life.*

*My shoes will be filled by someone with even smellier feet.*

*Someone who people might think actually existed even if it's just for a brief blink.*

*Will you slap me if I curse you?*

*Will you raise an eyebrow if I make a loud enough noise.*

*Will you look at me in my creaseless white Shabbos shirt or will you drip miniscule drops of grape juice and olive oil on it to push me deeper inside of my ego?*

*I don't know what you want from me God.*

*I don't know what to do to please you.*

*I don't even know what to do to anger you.*

*You are a mystery to me, and I am no Sherlock.*

*Do you have a joke up there 'how many Abies does it take?'*

*Are angels laughing at my stumbles.*

*Is there something that I'm missing here?*

*Will anyone peek behind the curtain for me.*

*God, where have all the eye glints gone?*

*Where were all those winks that told me that we're all just acting a part?*

*Is this not a play anymore?*

*Is this all actually for real now?*

*Or have we just gone so deep into our roles that we've forgotten who we are.*

*God, my grandfather used to be an angel.*

*He used to have wings that would make his feet hover all over the Synagogue.*

*Like a marionette he would move around the Shabbos table.*

*Even the tablecloth would support me when I didn't have the courage to continue.*

*Everyone used to be giddy.*

*Everyone used to be alive.*

*Fuck, God, none of us even got a proper funeral.*

We don't even get the decency for a grave and stumble around our lives with our very essence sucked out.

We can't breathe God.

Your children's cheeks are sticking into their mouths.

We are butt naked skeletons covering ourselves with layers and layers of fat.

Even global warming is trying to warm our frozen hearts.

There isn't even any greed anymore.

There are just starving people stuffing themselves with salty fish and dry air.

God, my selfishness knows no bounds.

I've lost the presupposition that I am somehow a good person.

My claim to valor is gone and with it my desire to be honorable.

*I give up God.*

*I resign to be just one of the crowd.*

*I join my brothers and sisters into death.*

*I join my brothers and sisters in the vein search for sense pleasures.*

*I will not stick out and be different.*

*I will mingle and be one of.*

*And when this world burns down, my hands will be just as dirty.*

*God, I don't understand this path you put me on.*

*I'm not as smart as your angels and cannot see further than yesteryear.*

*God, if you refuse to let me love you then it's your children who I will love.*

*I hereby separate myself from you and turn around into where I've always been.*

*This world might be empty, but it is full for the empty.*

*I will enjoy the simple pleasures and orient my life towards the pursuit of nothing.*

*God, if you see me at some corner not aware of reality.*

*If you see me under a scaffolding eating and drinking.*

*If you see me laughing with friends, blind to the possibilities of my surroundings.*

*If you see me about to fall into the lowest depth.*

*If you see me shake my fist or cough out a rotten tooth.*

*If you see me desperate for some dead end.*

*God, whenever you see me look at me closely.*

*Look at how small-minded I am.*

*Look at how oblivious my face is.*

*Look at how much I don't care about your potential.*

*Look at how much of what you have to offer I've given up on and think about the worth of your eternity.*

*Eternity is forever but all the now's that us humans get, they are pregnant with something way beyond the beyond.*

*God, I thank you for your offer of kindness, but I have to decline, my brother's wedding is tomorrow, and I have my cousin's Vach Nacht tonight.*

# Kneeling Down to Pray

A terrified man walks the streets of your town.

His walk is slightly erratic but to the untrained eye he looks like everyone else just scurrying about their day.

Were days this slippery ten years ago or is this all new?

My days used to be sticky and saturated in a way that only a good wash of Saturday could clean.

These days though, it feels as though none of can properly grab a hold of any day.

*God, what use is Saturday if there is no Wednesday?*

*What use is lubricant Sunday if there is no Monday?*

*What use am I in a meaningless world?*

*I used to live for something.*

*If I'd follow it until the end, it would probably be meaningless too, but it felt like something.*

*I felt like something.*

*God, I want to feel something.*

*God, I want to be alive again.*

*You've beaten the truth out of me, and I don't need it to be true, I just want something.*

*A calendar to lock me into normalized insanity.*

*I want to say again with fervor "I'm planning on" or "I'll do it tomorrow."*

*God, I've protested over my words, your words, their words and am left with tasteless food.*

*God, help me sell my soul to you.*

*I just want to be alive for you.*

*I want to read your Bible and cry a prayer for the hole in my heart disguised as a new love or nicer house.*

*God, with you even pizza could be salvation.*

*God, I want to hold a slice over my head.*

*Anoint me my God in your extracted mozzarella oil.*

*God, my love, I want my chest to pull me into synagogues and churches and bar fights and weddings and funerals and friends and closed-circuit thinking.*

*God, I'm alone, people don't have souls and my brain lost its connection to everyone else.*

*Even my dick doesn't know where to go anymore.*

*God, you've enriched my life and now there's no point.*

*God, I'm scared.*

*No one can tell but I'm terrified.*

*Everyone's in denial or maybe I'm in denial.*

*Were all stubborn blushing blind people wiping ourselves off at the bottom of staircases making sure no one saw.*

*We all have moments of weakness but even a misshapen ball keeps rolling.*

*God, save us.*

*God, you are now timeless.*

*Please, go back in time and stop us from creating you.*

*You enrich our lives too much and now we've forgotten about living.*

*Gratitude feels good on the exhale.*

*God, I don't want to be grateful.*

*I don't want to shove my protests down under my smile.*

*Umbrellas dispose of each drop quickly, so they don't have to be strong.*

*My shut mouth is ready to burst, every smile adding more pressure.*

Smiles feel good.

Gratitude feels good.

Love feels good.

Fear doesn't.

Pain doesn't.

Self-awareness doesn't.

Not knowing doesn't.

*God, I wish religions were true.*

*I wish with all my heart that they were the pathways to inner blossom.*

*I wish our brains opened ever so slightly with every smile and that our chest softened with every moment of gratitude.*

*I wish excitement wasn't just a contraction.*

*God, I'm so close to creating you again because being awake is so frightening.*

*God, I need a system to take care of some of the processes because it's hard for me to see it all in every moment.*

# Small Vision Expanded Veins

Theres a dear God effect that washes over me every month or so.

The day starts off with a slightly higher dose of dopamine which rises into the afternoon.

I often think of how many snacks I'd pack if I were a WWII bomber.

How far have I gotten lost in the softness of my pillows.

How I roll over and over swimming in the smooth and silky.

My socks are clean and my underwear still resemble themselves.

After lunch on my holy day, I can feel the air being pushed up and out of my body.

I can feel it getting stuck beneath my Adams apple forcing my eyes to bulge and my cheeks clench squeezing warm tears from my eyes.

My heart crumbles and I begin to say.

*Dear God, my heart can't handle the immensity of human suffering.*

*Dear God, my heart aches all day as I look at the worn-out faces of those I love.*

*God, they are all so lost as am I, but their pain is so much deeper.*

*Please God, show me beyond their wrinkles and frowns.*

*Push me beyond this moment for we are all trapped in our cells only capable of dreaming up wider cells.*

This pain eventually passes as the sun starts to set and my shoulders make their way back up then down into their sweet spot.

My Rabbi would do a dance move and make a lot of noise when something was too hard to explain.

Maybe the sunset firework show is god's noise, and the soft breeze is his dance passing around me.

It's at this point that my mind starts a wordless prayer that goes something like.

*God, it feels as though you want my heart to get colder.*

*That you want me to get used to human pain and close my heart a few millimeters every day.*

*God, could I invite you into my point of view?*

*Could I share with you the tragedies that I see daily?*

Today I saw the sternest face on a sixty-year-old man. I dared not keep looking but couldn't stop. His lips were pursed in protest as he felt a crash of anxiety because of the person in front of him's "clearly wrong decision." The top of his already enlarged face was protruding at the temples as he finally submitted with visual frustration, clenched teeth and no eye contact.

He cared so much about the person in from of him and felt like he was making the biggest mistake of his life and if he could just listen to him, he would be saved.

*God, you placed angels in prisons. You cast us into tight and narrow visions with hearts that keep on pumping pure blue blood into our expanding veins.*

*God, you've cut our wings and watch us crash over and over again into the sweetest ground turned hard rock.*

*God, in the words of the divine mothers around me I proclaim 'I can't. I just can't.'*

*Dear God, am I supposed to make myself comfortable in my cell? Should I keep standing or should I sit down? Should I look up or look into your blocked eyes all around me?*

*Why did you make us so pure and sweet and angry and loving and lost and arrogant and boastful?*

*Why did you trap us in these stories?*

*God, I'm so tired of acting. I'm so tired of smiling. I'm so tired of scratching my chest. I'm so tired of lifting my head up yet again. The 'fall seven get up eight' has worn my knees and the constant filtering might necessitate a new prostate.*

*God, this is all so beautiful and profound, but just once let's have a simple quiet night in with the drapes drawn.*

*God, Dear God, I'm so tired of walking off into the sunset.*

# A Day in The Life

Mistake.

I'm making a big mistake.

The wind is cold on my back, but my chest is on fire.

What is life anyhow?

We all walk around like we weren't just dropped into an absurd reality.

I respect our stubbornness and watch our stern faces holding out our biggest shit yet.

They say that the body releases its bowels during the death process.

The face, however, hardens cement rigor.

Some things we never let go of.

They are torn out of our hands, but our hands stay grasped.

*God, I'm tired.*

*I've fallen into the pit for many lifetimes this week.*

*I watched the clock never go past minute 59 and return all the way basck to zero.*

*I stayed up all night and saw that the sun rose ever so slowly.*

*God, I learned it all the hard way. I learned that there is no now.*

*That I'll never arrive.*

*God, I know it all now. I know what's real and what's not. I know it all as it truly is.*

*God, now is a good time to take me because I'm about to get sucked back in.*

*I'm about to forget it all and I don't know when I'll know again.*

*God, do you forget?*

*Do you fall into love?*

*Do you climb out of love covered in the entire world's filth?*

*God, I'm here again.*

*I'm staring you in the eyes covered in the world shit.*

*I can feel my eyes pulling me back into the pit of shame.*

*God, shame's a funny one. It crawls in the strings of your muscles. You can feel it tug at all the hairs all the way up, warping your brain into the ghosts of evil.*

*God, I don't know anymore.*

*My truth is gone as my muscles twitch on the dance floor.*

*God, I can no longer look at you in the eyes.*

*The filth of the world is no longer on me.*

*I am the filth.*

*If you see me walking crooked just know that I've ingested it all.*

*My pores never close and I don't perspire.*

*God, I'm tired but I don't know why.*

*This world is so beautiful.*

*The walls and creepy crawlers are all edible and taste amazing.*

*Is this some sort of cartoon fairytale?*

*People fall in love and their eyes sparkle like diamonds.*

*Parents hold their warm babies in their arms.*

*But God, why am I the only one happy?*

*Why are people's faces so sad?*

*Why can't they see how lovely this world is.*

*God, don't judge your children for not being grateful.*

*Don't look at their frowns because they just don't know.*

*God, listen to my prayer and the cleanliness of my heart.*

*They are all in the dark, but I see the truth.*

*People are good.*

*Life is good.*

*They just don't know that our evil isn't ours.*

*God, could I stay with you like this forever?*

*Could we just look at each other and live within ourselves knowing the truth of who we really are?*

*God, I'm falling asleep.*

*I'm sorry for forgetting you once again.*

*I'm sorry for not separating myself from myself.*

*God, I'll never forget this moment.*

*This is home.*

*This is love.*

*This is us.*

# Nothing To Protect

How quickly I forget about a toothache.

How I can feel it pulsate and splash pain all over my face.

Do tigers have toothaches?

Does it hurt because I chew or because I've hung my teeth beside my bow?

*God, physical pain wakes me up to reality.*

*When I'm in pain I am aware and present and tethered and here.*

I used to think that pain was painful.

That I would cry and kick and scream because the pain was too much.

I met the angriest man in the world a few years ago.

His smile stretched past his teeth, gum and even a few inches away from his face.

It was on accident that we shared more than just a passing glance.

He told me that he was the sweeper.

That he loved everyone so much.

As we stood there shining at each other it felt as if all the happiness of the world was filling us up through the holes in the feet of our pants.

I could feel my breath shorten and my stomach muscles push my chest up into the bottom of my jaw. My eyes started to moisten a bit and I could feel my forehead iron out my wrinkles.

What happened next seemed so abrupt and out of context. My stomach and chest contracted slightly pushing everything up with even more force sprouting the most beautiful smile on my face.

I could feel my skin illuminate as all of me became one with everything.

A shining star on a dying planet, I stood standing.

*Was that you, my God?*

*Are you real like they said you said you are?*

*God, please be real.*

*I want to be more than.*

*I want to be an angel.*

*I want to escape this earth after I'm wasted.*

*God, save me.*

*God, I'm scared.*

*The only times when I'm not scared are when I'm busy.*

*God, I don't think when I'm busy.*

*All religions seem to toe the line between rationale and beyond rationale pushing us into thoughts in thoughtlessness.*

*The busy man sins less.*

*Arbeit Macht Frei?!*

*God, I used to think that someone knew the truth, but I was just too stupid or broken or twisted or blocked to see it.*

*I know now that no one knows.*

*That when we lift our hands up and point it's because we don't know.*

*The conviction is convincing or is it the convincing is conviction.*

*God, how do I serve you if my prayers don't really face east?*

*God, how can I continue acting like I know when I know that I never will?*

*Is truth a real thing?*

*Does truth exist or does it only cancel out the nontruths?*

*In a world with no anger, would there be a truth to protect?*

*In a world with no smiles would anger be conceived.*

# Lie To Love

"He's a good eater." I heard my aunt tell my mother.

Highchairs are so uncomfortable.

The backrest is so far back that I need to crunch my whole stomach and quickly grab my food before flinging back.

No one ever smiles at each other.

I'm the only one that makes people smile.

I like watching my sister cry.

Her face becomes so bright and her skin starts shining.

It's hard to remember what it was like to be a baby but it's all there somewhere.

I knew as a baby; I just didn't know that there was knowing.

I remember the first time I learned about knowing.

I was standing outside my classroom stammering to my teacher about what had happened.

Stammering is like fishing. You stick your hand in and hope you pull something living out.

What had happened was simple but that won't get me out of my jail cell far away from the happiness of my class that I could still faintly feel.

*God, what is context?*

*What are giants and why do they look so friendly?*

I was still smart back then and sported a strong impenetrable face.

He became friendlier and friendlier the stronger I got.

I knew back then; I just didn't know that there was knowing.

My teacher started off as my teacher, then my friend and then my savior as he leaned over me scrunching a protruding object hanging from the bulletin board.

I took me years to process that day and what detour it created in my mind's method of operation.

He made a funny face and I laughed. Everything came crashing down and my stomach twisted. I walked back to my seat bewildered and spaced out most of the class for the rest of the year.

I had done something wrong.

I knew it but the teacher's eyes would now glint at me.

That day beneath his tree trunk hands I told my first manipulative lie.

I didn't know it, but I knew exactly what he wanted to hear and after cracking a smile, I was now part of his self-serving club.

He and I were now buddies.

We had an understanding that went beyond the truth.

We bonded and I proved to him that I knew what he wanted to hear and was willing to deliver.

My initial strong hesitation showed him that I had character and would be a strong addition to his team.

I was the most well connected second grader.

If you needed anything, I could get it done.

I could get the class to go onto the deck for recess or I could get us down to the gym and score points with the cool kids even though none of us could get the basketball anywhere near the hoop.

That pause and sparkle was a reminder of the wrong that I did.

But what wrong?

I knew back then; I just didn't know that there was knowing.

I didn't think much about it but that knot in my stomach never left.

*God, I don't want to have friends.*

*I don't want to be a part of your dirt.*

*I don't want to tell you what you want to hear.*

*God, I don't like being human.*

*I don't like having friendships, let alone memberships that are based on face reading and lying.*

*God, this experience is so convoluted.*

*At what point does it all go to shit?*

*Life used to be as simple as smashing against the highchair backrest with food twisted within my pudgy fingers.*

*How do I go back to watching and sitting and fat squishy face wheezing in some air in between bites?*

*God, all the people I love, I lie to.*

*God, I'm tired and ashamed of the life I lead and I don't know how to make it stop.*

*God, I want a reset.*

*I want a do over.*

*I want to have not laughed at my teacher's stupid joke.*

*God, I feel so dirty.*

*God I now understand generational shit.*

*I'm still covered with the greed from our journey out of Egypt.*

# Soul Plumbing

There are many wonders in this world.

Some of these wonders are peace and war, hate and disgust, spite and greed, and love and hunger.

I used to feel disgusting when I felt disgust.

I would feel relaxed in a place of peace.

I would feel lovely within the folds of love.

I would walk into rooms and soak it all in, usually, leaving me at the door.

“Doors are funny things” said the door hinge as he clapped for the newcomer.

In the Hasidic *Breslov* tradition, clapping is used in prayer to ward off evil inclinations.

On the high holidays in a *Breslov* Synagogue the clapping almost feels like applause.

Is the hinge clapping for me?

Am I being warded off?

Am I evil?

What’s happening in the room right now?

I kind of like the feeling of sitting on the steps outside.

It’s so warm in the cold.

It’s so clear within convoluted contempt.

Why am I always left at the door only to have to find my own way home.

Why does my food always dangle so loosely?

*God, I'm here again with you.*

*God, this world keeps on exploding in my face.*

*God, there are so many words and feelings and emotions that I'm completely blocked.*

Plungers only make a bigger mess and I feel as though it's all for naught.

I stayed in a cabin one summer.

The toilet clogged all the way down the pipe towards the septic tank.

The water would eventually go down, but the rest wouldn't and by the end of the summer it was almost cement strong.

When you're fighting an infection, your face looks the same.

Tears are so silent and translucent.

Nose scrunches relieve itches and panicked triple gasps of air make it all go away.

*God, could you make it all away.*

*Dribble my tears down my face, scrunch my nose and shove air into my lungs in rapid succession because there's nothing left in me.*

*God, I'm an emotional cripple.*

*I need a plumber to come and clear me up.*

*I need someone to carry my heart down the stairs and into the kitchen so that I could make myself a coffee.*

*God, I want more and less.*

*My experience is a polarized one following the limited horizon of one point of view's vision.*

*God, I don't need to land anymore.*

*I allow myself to be left out at parties and social functions and welcome myself back into myself when I eventually come home frazzled and wanting.*

*God, I've accepted my life.*

*Will you accept it too?*

# I Can Do It All By Myself

I'm leaving behind my dreams of fitting into my old group of friends.

I'm leaving behind a hope that someone out there knows the truth.

I'm leaving behind my want to be a better person who will lead a good life.

I'm leaving behind my desire for money.

I'm taking with me a beautiful hope that I am good enough and my life is right for me.

I'm taking with me a leap of faith that I know what's best for me.

I'm taking with me a desire to listen and allow for humbleness to reside within me.

*God, why do I hate you so much?*

*Why is all of my attention fixated on the small part of me that you have a hold on?*

*God, I hate you with all my heart.*

*I can feel your hold on me ever since I dropped my first candy on carpeted floor.*

*I remember working for ever trying to get the hair off it.*

*I even tried to lick parts of it but had to wash my tongue and it felt itchy until after my eyes closed that night.*

*I remember how many little thingies I found on my tongue and rushed to the bathroom to see what they were.*

*I used to accept things as they are.*

*I used to explore the sides of my room with my toy car and bump off a corner when I hit one.*

*No more god.*

*I don't accept any of this!*

*I don't want you to hold me anymore.*

*I want to follow the invisible.*

*I want to follow the rain down and not twist release after it has accumulated.*

*God, you give me sustenance.*

*You gave me my food today and last Tuesday.*

*You showed me strength and agility.*

*You showed me how to hold ground.*

*You showed me how to stretch deep beneath and squiggle my way into an existence.*

*You showed me the weak and how they topple.*

*You showed me the power of the collective and how one replaces the other.*

*God, you've shown me wisdom and courage and how to have a backbone in a baren land.*

*You brought me from a raindrop and carried me up and up and out and sprout.*

*God, I am forever in debt to you and respect the richness of your heritage.*

*I love the way you sway as the moon shines its beam into a ray.*

*How your soft song can only be heard in unison and how it can lift even the heaviest heart.*

*God, your way is beautiful but it's your way.*

*Not mine.*

*My way.*

*My way is yet to unfold.*

*My untold involves devolving into the brightest of reds.*

*My orange will fly and roll and toss and crunch.*

*My end is crunch, my god.*

*My end is dust.*

*My end is quaint.*

*My end is quick.*

*My end is anticlimactic.*

*But that's my end.*

*It's my end.*

*Mine.*

*Also beautiful.*

*Also a song.*

*Also filled with strength and valor.*

*My end is also free, oh so free my God.*

*That wind that blows through your floor.*

*That same wind will hold me in its arms and cradle me.*

*I will be your song my God.*

*I will blow through you.*

*I will be the song within your forest choir.*

*God, my is mine*

*My end is now.*

*My now is mine*

*And my God today as we separate, we truly become one.*

# Party Planning

Stale breath doesn't bother me.

I lean in close as perfect fades to pure.

They talk about how time stops when you're in love.

Time doesn't stop, it changes.

Space changes too and so does being.

What doesn't change, though, is the slow residual grinding of the heart valves against themselves.

An itch in that hard-to-reach spot where the soul meets the spirit.

Most people don't notice it in the initial phase when smiles intertwine with the ears and forehead.

But the shoulders shrug ever so slightly, and the arm muscles start to stretch and wind up behind the neck.

Oh the neck, that one and only.

The lover who loaned their jaw to the head above it.

The one who only exists as an avenue to facilitate a union of consumption and utilization.

Oh neck, I pray with you.

I sit erect, perched on my hovering mountain of a planet.

God gave the Torah on the smallest of mountains, oh neck.

So why is it so hard to believe that he gave it in you.

My drunken Rabbi would speak of how this world is just a preparation for the next.

This is one heck of an event we must be creating.

What do you think the theme of your party is?

It's got to be some sort of transportation event.

I met a party planner who suggested people start planning their event six months in advance.

Her events last about five hours.

Will my party be five hours?

Will we go from the atrium into the repurposed greenhouse decked out in pink and white?

Will my eyes flash at the party goers as I cordially sway past them.

Will there be a rhythm in heaven?

What will the tempo be like?

*God, I've walked your earth and tried all there seems to be.*

*I've tasted the richest of thoughts and drank the thickest of your waters.*

*I've stood on mountaintops and caressed the finest of woods.*

*I've been weak and strong.*

*I've been loud and wrong.*

*I've felt the entire universe flow through my still body.*

*God, I've done it all.*

*What's left for me now?*

*Do I shuffle and repeat, or do I search for something else that I might have missed.*

*God, I speak of you to my windshield on long drives between stories.*

*I tell of your richness and buoyant nature.*

*I cook delicacies out of the different parts of you and share how lucky we are to be here.*

*God, I'm a good mixologist.*

*I can get the giddy drunk on your fermented shit.*

*I can lie really well like you taught me to.*

*I can tell myself that I believe in good and evil.*

*That I stand for right and wrong...*

*Until...*

*Until I become human again and greed lines my eyelids.*

*Oh my eyelids, God.*

*Why did you let me spoil my eyelids.*

*I wish that bags grew in the place of purple and pink.*

*I wish that my face morph twirled into twist.*

*God, how can I smile at those I meet when I'm holding my face straight.*

*How can I tell one story with my face and another with my words.*

*Those who truly listen can only hear with their eyes.*

*A face tells a thousand stories.*

*A story tells a thousand lies with me.*

*God, Nachshon Ben Aminadav ran into the ocean.*

His action was a lie against his body.

He inspired us all to run and dive.

There's a silence that comes over a room when everyone locks onto the same mission at the same moment.

There a clarity of eyesight and blood vessels open wide allowing it all to gush through.

*God, what is being asked of me?*

*Am I being called to lie?*

*Am I supposed to ignore and dive?*

*Is it any lie or are there specific ones that you want me to incorporate?*

*Do you see my white flag blowing through your wind?*

*Did you see me stretch out my mask to dry last night?*

*I give in.*

*I give up.*

*I'm open.*

*I'm available.*

*I'm ready to cover all mirrors with you.*

*I'm ready to hide myself behind you.*

*God, thank you.*

*God, I'm alive.*

*God, I'm pulling up my anchor and ready to say adrift.*

*God, I proclaim.*

*Let it rain.*

*Let's get lost in your world with no agenda.*

*Let's get drunk on your water and sway wildly as we pray the night away.*

# Let Go, Hold On and Let Go

He asked me for a ride home again.

He asked me which route I take to get home and confirmed that I pass by his house.

My face tensed up into a smile and I told him that I'd have to think about it.

The toothless man that I work with whose stench lines my still working nostril.

I can often smell him randomly on my bed late at night as another one of his crystals get absorbed into my mucous membrane as it continues moisturizing my nose.

*God, I want to help everyone.*

*I want to hold a napkin under the mouths of sloppy soup eaters.*

*I want to umbrella my coat over that chubby old lady swaying herself west to east up the narrowing street.*

*I want to hug and snuggle terrored eyes.*

*I want to sing and dance and flip back over all the upside-*down *tables in people's houses.*

*Like a clown, God.*

*Like a goddam clown I want to smush all the faces.*

*I want to confuse the masses back to sanity, God.*

Confusion in this world is doubt.

Confusion in the next is freedom.

Freedom from knowing.

Freedom from slavery.

Freedom from the angry mob in one's head trying to make sense of it all.

Life, we call it, this lack of life we find ourselves in.

I watch people connected to their machine body, sapping all their energy until the end when the soul is nearly extinguished.

I watch particularly old people whose souls are on their last breath and wonder if their soul will be free before it suffocates.

Old people have resilient souls.

The dead young ones have pure souls that can't stand losing their light.

They feel their soul dying and hop out of their machine.

Hell is nothing compared to what's happening here on earth.

I watched an anorexic girl smile.

I saw her bones move and wanted to bow before her.

She would die not long after that, freeing her soul and avenging the attempted murder.

My friend from school later became anorexic too.

She was said to have flung her shit at her friends who were trying to help her.

She was going the other way.

Avenging her soul for plaguing her body.

Avenging her soul for tormenting her with guilt.

*I'm confused God.*

*Do I worship you or am I also going in the wrong direction?*

*There are two people praying side by side in a temple heading in completely different directions.*

*God, you told me that the why doesn't matter.*

*You told me that if I just acted good then I'd be good.*

*I'm not good God.*

*My instrument is faulty and taking me deeper into my hungry body.*

*Fuck, God, what's there to do in this world?*

*Are we all just serving our devil bodies.*

*God, what's this all about?*

*At what point will I give up and leave my body behind?*

*If I know the ending, then do I still need to hear the whole story?*

*Haven't I heard enough God?*

*Haven't I attacked my soul enough.*

*Do I need my skin to thin?*

*For my bones to brittle under the weight of my oversized head?*

*For my head to cower into the ground under the weight of thousands of wasted-life punchline jokes?*

*For my toenails to turn into thick tree bark and stick up under my punctured slippers?*

*God, I don't see the point in living anymore.*

*I've done it all twice and you know the third is cliché.*

*God this seems tasteless.*

*How many times could I wake up to the same nightmare?*

Aren't you bored by this, oh mighty god of thunder and lightning.

Zap me God.

Zap me back into myself, because I don't know if I could ignore the souls around me anymore.

Are we only allowed to notice the anorexics, business jumpers and wrist-slitted fags?

What about the rest of us who are just barely alive inside?

What about those sad faces treasuring inaccessible eternal joy eighteen inches beneath the souls of their hearts?

Fuck, God.

I want to roar my soul out of my stretched-out throat.

I want fuck all this shit up.

*God, like a drunk I want to dance on top of the table.*

*I want to slap and slap until I see that glimmer again.*

*I want to pull people out of their infinitely layered lives.*

*God, when was the last time you saw someone really dance?*

*I don't mean dance to the rhythm of a song.*

*I don't mean jumping up and down or holding a beloved close above a mountain of your collected lives.*

*I mean dancing, God.*

*Dancing to no song*

*To no music or sounds.*

*Dancing from an expanding heart*
*pushing tears of joy up through the eyes.*

*Dancing with a loose smile that drops*
*once the tension smiles and frowns have*
*gone through all their protests.*

*God, I want to see people dancing.*

*Please God, let us stretch a moment a*
*mile wide and fill it with all your*
*emaciated souls gasping for fresh air.*

*God, an angel once told me to hold on*
*tight.*

*He came back later on and told me to let*
*go.*

*Five years after that he told me to hold on and today, he told me to look him in his eye.*

*Beyond it all I'm left anger-less and alone.*

*There are no answers here, only better questions.*

*God, on that faithless day beyond his fiery eye I saw the truth.*

*I saw that letting go is holding on too.*

*That as a human I'm left with no other option than to hold on, let go and then let go of letting go.*

*God, I don't have a request at this point only that I may one day see my heart as it's meant to be.*

*I want my soul to survive this inferno of a life and be able to nurse itself back to the beauty of that vibrant angel it once was.*

*God, thank you for my confusion and please God, please don't let me forget who I truly am.*

# Unguarded Treasure

There are eighteen people cramped in my room at night as I sleep.

That is eighteen plus me, so I guess fifty-two.

Yesterday I wanted ice cream.

Today, I want meat.

Tomorrow I'll want something, but it definitely won't be the first two.

*God, do you like ice cream me better than meat me?*

*Do you like how he fills your lines with sweetness?*

*How the bitterness of his soul craves your honey?*

*Am I too rugged for you?*

*Does my meaty contentment bother you?*

*Are you offended by my lackadaisical attitude as I sit in solitude?*

*Or*

*Or God, do I crave ice cream when that's what you are?*

*Do you go through your own shifts where one day you shine one way and on another you don't shine at all?*

*God almighty!*

*I'm on my hands and knees here beneath your moody world.*

*I've sat here through rain, sleet and muddy hearts.*

*I've scrubbed through pain and plight and mornings delight.*

*And yet...*

*And yet my sun doesn't shine.*

*My sun burns but gives no light.*

*My sun is radioactive and only glows when I'm asleep.*

*God, I've watched the whole world turn against me.*

*I stood there and watched faces laugh and taunt me.*

*I've watched jealous women plot against me.*

*I stood there, head up and back straight, accepting it all.*

*I would be getting a beating once I hung my role up and left work.*

*They would surround me and teach me a lesson.*

*A lesson for what, God?*

Where has this word lesson come from?

Do we need to learn in order to live?

What is learning and why are we doomed if not for it?

A blind man once walked me home from school.

He had nothing to do, and I hadn't learned the word no yet.

He spoke about his loved ones who were few and far.

He told me what they each smelled like in great detail and said that the ones who smelled the worst he felt the strongest connection to.

I showed him how long I could balance a stick on my finger.

I told him I could go on forever and threw the stick down letting it bounce on the floor a few times until it rolled away.

He would meet me daily and walk me the two long scary blocks on the main street.

I showed how I would fly if I could and helped him shape his hands in a way that would allow him to direct himself once airborne.

He told me that I was a treasure.

I asked him if I needed to be kept in a safe.

He said that some treasures can't be hidden.

I asked him why he's blind.

He told me that some treasures had to be hidden.

I asked him how long he will be blind for.

He rattled his dog and gave him a treat.

The street looked empty without him.

My brain looks empty without him.

I need someone that I could ask questions to.

I need a friend who doesn't need me.

I need to be free to be me.

*God, you've built a layered world here and I'm caught in the middle of it.*

*I seem to only be of importance if I stick to my layer.*

*But I refuse.*

*I don't know why but I think it's my mission to spill into all the layers of your world.*

*I'm to burn into the lava and freeze into space.*

*I'm to soak my skin wet and crack dry in the desert.*

*God, my layer is not enough for me.*

*This life is not enough for me.*

*Fuck money and valor and strength and strategy.*

*I will kick and scream and won't leave without my toy.*

*God, don't fight me in this world.*

*Let me be how I want to be.*

*Trust me because I don't trust myself.*

*Allow me to flourish and drill until I spill.*

*I'm not connected to myself so don't be either.*

*God, if I'm to be a treasure then I'm the kind that can't be guarded.*

# The Game of God

He asked me what anger felt like.

He asked me why the left side of my face was twitching.

He asked me why my arms were caressing each other.

He asked me why I keep massaging my neck.

Why my breath was shallow.

Why my heart was skipping forward.

Why my nose kept squishing in.

Why my eyes darted up up and away.

Why my right eye was hiding in the corner.

Why my foot rubbed the clear smooth floor beneath.

Why my socks were slipping off.

Why my forehead collected my skin between my eyebrows.

Why my face looked angelic.

Why my demand was just but my tone was exaggerated, demanding and unwavering.

Why I looked as though I wanted to bite my own head off.

Why I kept on swearing in the name of a god who I've denounced publicly and in the deepest crevasse of my heart.

*God, it's been a few hours since I've lost myself into the world of anger.*

*I feel cleansed god.*

*I feel like my anger washed the soul in my body and rebooted existence within me.*

*God, what is anger?*

*What is greed, God?*

*Why do I need to forget to remember?*

*Why do I need to destroy to create?*

*God, every day I walk by the third street bench from the corner of my street.*

*As I walk by, we exchange our knowledge for that day.*

*He tells me tales of destruction as he coughs out carbon from his part mummified body.*

*He squeezes smiles between bolts holding the wrong sides of him together.*

*Yesterday he told me that he could feel the moisture of the earth thin out into a light gas.*

*He yells loudly with his thick trailing voice and sings of a past with rich manure and delicious air.*

*I listen to him day in and day out as he spills his soul.*

*When it's my turn to speak, I say the same report to him every day. "Death is only slow because life has already begun to grow within in it."*

*God, I vouch for your chaos every day as I put my shoulders on, one arm at a time.*

*I walk your world with my seeing-eye-smile leading my way through this wilderness.*

*People walk silently around your world.*

*They walk up and down the same streets every day and meet their version of a street bench.*

*They all listen attentively to what it has to say, and all repeat the same line to it before opening the doors to their houses.*

*We believe God.*

*We believe in you.*

*We believe in this world.*

*We fight for your vision.*

*We fight for your name.*

*We point weapons at each other so that we can profess our love to you.*

*A staged act where everyone is right, and the victor gets to share your vision.*

*God, people are dying right now.*

*People are scared.*

*People are alone.*

*People want to release a deep breath before getting into bed.*

*But people are people and people are angry.*

*And people are greedy.*

*And people believe.*

*People believe in you, God, but there are seventy vantage points to your name.*

*God, we want to kill seventy nations to proclaim your name.*

*We want to create life within death.*

*We want to be right, so we create a wrong to enforce our right.*

*God, games are made when two entities decide on a means of communication and abide by those rules.*

*We are playing with each other, so our world is lopsided.*

*God, look within each of our hearts.*

*Look into our left ventricles and see that our personal game is simple and pure.*

*We know what we know but get confused when we hear other ways of seeing life, of seeing you.*

God, every interaction is sacred.

Buying food is a proclamation.

Buying food is speaking out the glory of being alive in this vibrant world.

Holding a leaf is being a part of the pulsating micros and macros making their way from life to life.

Seeing a smile burst out of a frowning face like a waterfall, is like seeing an angel come to life in the dead of space.

God, I see faces gushing with your pride everywhere I go.

Their faces gleam and glisten out of the darknesses of their confusions.

God, I hope I've buttered you up for a request because I'd like to ask for one thing.

*Please let all the people of this world remember who they are with clarity and conviction so that all our pain and differences can melt between our cracks.*

*Please God, help this world heal itself back up and blossom once again into the peachy green, blue and white paradise it once was.*

*God, I want to keep biting into apples and chomping down grapes so please God plant our souls with the clarity of all your names and let us sing together and bask in your glory.*

*Amen!*

# The Maternal God

An angel once walked among us.

He had broad shoulders and an ax shaped face.

Two guards accompanied him holding glistening golden polished pitchforks.

The tips of the blades curled thin into the unseen.

My friend's father described this scene as everyone's floodlights tied their hopes and dreams to his shining face.

I remember seeing the mother's face beaming with pride as she faced her children, tying her hopes and dreams onto each one of them.

When her eyes left Yerucham they landed on my face and a soft smile lifted her lips before returning her attention to the radiating man.

After that Shabbos, I never fully left that house.

I would find any excuse to end up there.

I loved the strict mother who put us to bed way too early and the way her food tasted bad.

I would lay on the pull-out bed near Yerucham's bed and fall asleep almost smiling her.

I became the best helper and hopped to the kitchen for napkins and cups.

I soaked it all in and let my mind blow me away.

Dad wasn't always shining like on that first Shabbos.

He was a stern man who had great demands.

His voice slammed into walls and feet raced up and down staircases by the wind of his huff.

Only Dad said no, and no one ever dragged their feet.

Then Sunday night would come, and it would be time to go home.

The house got quiet as mom sat outside Yerucham's room and I waited for someone to pick me up.

There was no dust on the floor and the lights were all facing me.

I already called ten times and mom told me that she was almost there and that I shouldn't call again.

It's so cold outside but my face is sticking out through the front door looking for her car's headlights, with my coat tucked under my armpit.

"She always does this" I think as a tear trails down my frozen cheek. "She's never going to show up."

"Come on Mommy!"

"It's been like half an hour, and you said a few minutes."

"Why can't you just be here already?!"

"Mommy, I just want to go home."

"Please just come Mommy"

"Please"

Each passing pair of headlights twisted my stomach, and my eyes burned as I wiped off the streaming tears with my plastic coat.

I can't go back into the house; I can't stop crying and Yerucham's mom can't see how much I'm hurting because of my mother.

"Please mommy, come already."

I start to panic and hide my face in the doorway as a scary stranger walks by, giving me a second look.

I stand under the door post between the warmth of a now foreign land and nowhere and start to pray.

*Hashem, my God, please make my mother show up already.*

*I didn't mean to push Mushka last week.*

*She just makes me so angry, and I couldn't help myself.*

*Please save me Hashem.*

*I need to go home.*

*Please Hashem, I'm so cold.*

I say as my thighs touch together and feel how frozen they both are.

*I'll be good Hashem. I promise!*

*Please hashem bring her here!*

*I just want to be home already.*

*Why can't you just bring her?!*

*Please hashem.*

I start saying *Shir Hama'alos* like my Rabbi told our class to do when we need something from God and promise myself that when I'm done it, her car will arrive.

My throat is starting to choke at this point and my wet face feels like it's a rock that's not part of my body.

Suddenly I see a car at the end of the street and my whole body tenses as I start to realize that this one could really be my mother.

Adrenaline floods my system, and I can barely contain myself.

I shriek quietly into the house that I'm leaving and run into the back seat of my mother's car.

Mommy is on the phone, so I try to make myself comfortable on the boxes as we drive away.

*God, I remember another trapped extended moment of innocence dealt a silent blow and ask you this.*

*Creator, my god and the god of my mother.*

*What would Rashi's commentary be on this story?*

*Would he show the beauty of the father, and mother?*

*Would he vilify my mother and turn me into a martyr?*

*God, I'm not here for the theatrics.*

*I'm not a character playing an act in a play.*

*This is very real to me!*

*Every breath I take is between life and death.*

*I don't know of an afterlife and my body doesn't believe that there is one.*

*God, I'm here now as then in the cold, drenched in tears and waiting for my mother.*

*I'm waiting in vain.*

*I'm waiting for the sake of waiting.*

*My mind is on fire and every false hope set of headlight twists me back into the omega of shame blowing this world round.*

*God, you robbed me of my innocence.*

*You did something that you deserve a whack for, since that's the way I'd love a friend who has done something like that.*

*God, somehow you still keep me wanting you and I'm conflicted with this codependent and abusive relationship we find ourselves in.*

*God, I love you more than anyone in this world and can barely muster up the courage to say these most loving words I have here for you.*

*God,*

*God,*

*Goodbye God*

# Cuddling Stars

Burly men used to wrap a calf around their shoulders when it was too tired to continue.

Frisky women used to flash a calf on their way to being pinned down for the night.

There was an angel who was said to house the original pair of socks created for the fragile son of a Pharaoh.

The socks didn't snuggle but wrapped around both legs creating a little baby bundle.

Jacob was sandwiched between rock and ladder.

I am sandwiched between time and matter.

I kick and scream as time whisks me away.

Space is three-dimensional.

Time is non-dimensional but one directional.

Time owns space and commands it within its ability to be non-structural.

My rabbi, while leaning on the swinging fence on the west side of our yeshiva roof explain to me that angels were necessary because there needs to be some semblance of an ego for matter to be able to gather and formulate itself.

My Rabbi liked talking about how empty angels are.

He would slam his table and tell us how lucky we are to be human.

He compared angel fixation to someone who wants to live their life repeating their wedding day over and over.

When he said it, I pictured a wedding cake and eating it over and over again day after day.

Is that why we can't say gratitude through *The Hallel* every day, but only on special occasions?

Will we miss the point?

I mean, what's wrong with living the wedding day over and over again?

Why do I hate cake after the third piece when the first one made my mouth all tingly?

*God, I want to be an angel.*

*I want to fly high and feel the whole world inside me.*

*I want to sing a song that flowers my heart, connecting me to all the happiness and meaningful suffering that this world has ever had.*

*I want my breath to be taken from me and to barely be able to squeeze my words due to the excitement.*

*I want to sway like the waves and rumble with the currents.*

*I want to explode over mountains and drip lava, creating new floating islands.*

*I want my beard to drift downwards and swirl into lead covered forests.*

*I want to stretch back feeling the tightness of my enchanted stomach.*

*I want to smash a brick with my forehead and knit a garment while rocking in a silent prayer.*

*I want to feel the bling splash and clatter of egos parading themselves through this blue and green planet we've rolled ourselves into.*

*God, even clouds are see-through from up close, how much more so our oozing organs.*

*God, we contrast black and white on our wedding day, how much more so on our day of reckoning.*

*Will you wear white on our day to match my deep black?*

*Will you sparkle into my void, showing off my straight and narrow?*

*God, I'm an angel too you know.*

*Sometimes, when everything clicks, I can feel my soul soar up into the heavens above.*

*I can feel the lightness of the human condition and how beautiful it all is.*

*I can see smiles bend into rainbows around sparkling teeth.*

*I can see how lumber crumbles to dust that we breathe into our inverted treeing lungs.*

*How each ventricle opens sucking in the various molecules of decay and sprouts alike.*

*How dry and wet combine without losing any of their essence.*

*God, I don't fit into nature.*

*I keep on losing who I am and am replaced by what preceded it.*

*God, if I whither, who will I be?*

*What will be left of me as I'm stripped away?*

*God, I used to love people.*

*I would listen with my chest muscles clenched, hanging on every word.*

*I would fall apart when I heard bad news and fracture for months on end.*

*I loved loving.*

*It felt so deep to be alive.*

*Now, though, I'm strong, oh how strong I've become.*

*I can stand straight and march on as though the fabric of reality hasn't completely deformed itself in the last few years.*

*I don't recognize my father who sits scrolling atop his stagnant empire.*

*Or my sister whose nervous system is so strained that her body has ordered her depression to be taken thrice seasonally.*

*Or my barber whose fight against his hunch turns his face looking like he had a botched facelift as he stretches his head back and up.*

*God, an angel walks among us.*

*God, angels walk among us.*

*Beautiful men and women perched on top of the mountains of their struggles.*

*God, people tell stories.*

*They light fires in the dark and curl up with each other shining hope round the circle.*

*God, most of world is lava, then there's water, then there's land, then there are living beings scattered around, then there are humans living mostly in cities stacked one on top of the other.*

*I thought that bunk beds were for kids but as I close my eyes, I say goodnight to all the neighbors whose beds are directly above mine.*

*God, we aren't like you spreading stars light-years apart.*

*You scatter us and we gather.*

*Each time we're displaced we find ourselves back in our homes surrounded by more of us.*

*God, I used to search for you among the trees.*

*I don't look for you anymore, God.*

*I sit among the stars as we sing our songs deep into the darkness enveloping us.*

# The Silent Feast

Rolling balls.

Shining halls.

Bottle clinks.

Bright smiles.

Dark kinks.

*God, why do such sensitive souls need so much pressure to know that they're being loved.*

*She wants to be choked, gaged, held down and spat on all to feel the care that's already there.*

*God, in this world there are great distances.*

*We stand miles away from the person closest to us.*

I speak extra loud to my grandmother who's hard of hearing.

She told me how lonely life gets once the hearing starts to go.

How a full room of loved ones becomes miles and miles long and how you can only really hear your own thoughts.

I've watched her over the past few years gradually space out at the head of the table.

First, she would ask questions and then eventually just sat there quietly.

I feel like she never saw my face until recently.

When we speak one on one, her judgment and fears for my well-being spill out of her like an eroded damn collapsing.

Her words come out of her mouth without leaving any reserve air in her lungs.

I can feel her upper body contract as if she sees a gorilla towering behind me.

But not here, now, with all this noise around her pushing her deep down under.

She lifts her head and looks around a room of loud silent people posing and stuffing their oval faces with colorful food.

*God, you've made my inner world so noisy.*

*I sit in silent rooms not able to hear my own thoughts.*

*You've made me hard of thinking.*

*I can't distinguish between the different octaves of the voices who keep on interrupting each other.*

*Is my condition supposed to bring me closer to the world around me in the same way that my grandmother's made her become her own best friend?*

*What are you trying to make me see God?*

*What am I missing here?*

*God, I don't like the way you open people's eyes in this world.*

*You prescribe cancer in the same manner that an overworked doctor prescribes antibiotics.*

*There's a Chinese curse "my you be born in an interesting time."*

*You've cursed every second of my life with happenings.*

*You've filled every crevice of my vision with hopelessness and doubt until I lay motionless like Jona in the belly of a pregnant whale barreling through waves.*

*God, you've given me a heavy workload with a weak processor.*

*Am I supposed to crash every few months and climb back out of my earthquake mind with sparking youthful eyes only to be torn back down again just as I get some footing?*

*How long do you think my smile will not be resentful?*

*How many more times do you think that my smile will sprout before it too will be bashed up and twisted?*

*God, I keep on volunteering myself into truth.*

*I leave my homeland and trek out into the unknown cleaning my heart over and over again.*

*I've given up the path in life.*

*I've given up ever knowing.*

*I've given up even needing to believe.*

*God, I don't want anything from you.*

*I don't want your smiles or pain.*

*I don't want your lessons or your gains.*

*Leave me alone God and let me just be unbothered within the flourishing desert of my soul.*

# Moving Lips

Plain taste.

Mangled chaste.

Muffled silence.

Loud embrace.

There were three entrances to the main Villinus Synagogue with the last one only known to few.

Children told stories of ghosts and witches and would place bets on who could get the closest.

I remember knowing where everything was in my house.

Now I can barely find my keys.

*God, I used to be curious and therefore knew a lot.*

*Now though, the excitement is gone, and all the tastes have already been tasted.*

*Death is the only flavor I haven't tried yet, but it probably just tastes like lavender and a sinking stomach.*

*God, what are angels if not replicas.*

*What does this world have to offer aside from a bootleg copy.*

*My brain spits out chemicals whose doses I've already experienced, and my face has ship-shaped in all directions.*

*Women taste slightly different but even that can get old.*

I met an old fairy on the corner of my block while running away from my house party.

Her smile looked heavier than her luggage which she kept on tripping over.

I don't have much luggage, but I trip over my smile daily.

It twists around my face like a loose and worn-out rope.

My Rabbi told me that lips are sacred and that our words never actually leave our lips.

*God, my lips are in constant prayer with you.*

*I can feel my childhood cries still shake the very ground I sleep on.*

*I could feel it fracture ahead of my steps and flip trees and stones and mud and homes.*

*I am doomed God, nothing will ever change.*

*The past is spilling into the future and the future is too scared to come out.*

*God, I keep spilling all over the place.*

*My rationale is sticky with intuition and my heart is covered in out-of-toon songs.*

*God, am I supposed to keep my composure or am I to be honest because honestly there is nothing composed about me.*

*I smile and frown and laugh and cry before I'm even done with my morning stretches.*

*God, do angels also lack harmony when they sing to you or is it all perfect?*

*What color is perfect because last I checked there were no actual colors as each one melds into the other.*

*If time were to stop, would it be at the end of a second or ten, a minute or three quarters of a year?*

*God, you've given me a broken brain.*

*My brain splits time and colors, and pudgy rain drops into crosslined molecules.*

*I've even split my songs into intros, verses, bridges, outros, choruses, hooks, refrains, breaks, solos and interludes.*

*God, how far have I traveled from reality?*

*Sometimes, I don't understand the words that I say.*

*God, I want to smile to you.*

*Just one smile would do it.*

*A moment where I can allow for all my truths to align into the next dimension.*

*God, I'm so tired of flipping switches all the time.*

*I'm tired of forgetting and I'm tired of remembering.*

*God, can there be one truth even if it's just for a day?*

*Can I have one conversation with you without wanting the exact opposite a moment later.*

*The Rambam talks about how everything in the human life is a balance.*

*It sure as hell doesn't feel balanced or at least you really enjoy the swing.*

*God, am I swinging high enough for you?*

*Do you love how far I travel in between realities?*

*Do you soak in the intensity of my laugh along with my cry?*

*What do you want from me and am I doing a good job?*

*I want a compliment, God.*

*I want you to tell me that all of this makes sense somehow, someway, somewhere.*

*God, please tell me that my broken heart translates into some beautiful flower in some other place because here it's just my twisted stomach filled with acid and bile.*

*God, I don't need answers or questions or words or songs. I just want to know that you can feel the love behind my bursting blood vessels.*

*I want you to know that my swelling face and bulging eyes are because my body can't contain this level of love for you.*

*God, thank you for this gift of life that you've given me.*

*Thank you for my aching heart and rageful body.*

*Thank you for the air I breathe and how my lungs roll out all the way down into the depths of hell.*

*Thank you for green mountains and yellow apples.*

*And above all God, thank you for putting so much effort into making sure that this world makes absolutely no sense.*

*Sincerely yours*

*Just another human.*

# The Silent Woman

Why do women freeze up during sex?

What happens in that pretty pretty mind that it all just goes blank?

Women are comfortable in vain.

Men deny their vanity.

He beats his chest to the rhythm of his denial.

"Fuck the world!"

His face mangles into a roar.

Her face can only twist into disgust.

We all have our weapons.

Subtleties are her domain.

Massive shifts are mine.

Surrounded by subtleties I slouch in the corner sharpening my arms for a day that'll never come.

My eyes are dead and have begun their descent into old age.

Like my grandfather's silent twenty-year journey from sparkle to glint and finally resting in a shimmering glimmer.

*God, my powers are useless.*

*I'm lost in a world of sensitivity with coarse skin and a calloused tongue.*

*You've plopped me down into the here and now and I spin with this lopsided world upward and away.*

*God, matter seems to bend space.*

*It forces few into one, causing all kinds of chaos.*

*God, you've placed many agendas into me and now I'm living in chaos.*

*She pushes me to notice but my goodness pulls me upward and away.*

*God, I don't want to feel.*

*I don't want to go through my psyche with a lice comb.*

*I don't want to live under a microscope.*

*God, I am scope.*

*My abilities are macro and pulled far beyond today, a year from now or a light-year from now.*

*This world means less to me than my spirit which stretches beyond the beyond.*

*On a clear day in the spirit world, I can feel the impetus for the big bang wrap around my spine for a millennium.*

*God, this life looks real, but we all know deep down that something's off.*

*That there's no way we could get that pulled into to the momentary life and death drama which like a camel's prickly tongue lick our salty faces.*

*God, you've given us the Bible in story format.*

*My respect for you lies in your respect for time.*

*God, what is it about time that you treat it so well?*

*Why do you roll the red carpet out for it but fuck space into a dark alleyway?*

*Does time have a brighter future?*

*Does it shine it's pretty face at you causing your knees to buckle?*

*God, am I your alleyway fuck?*

*Will you leave me the second it's time?*

*I'm cramped here God.*

*You've compressed all of me into a diamond and then compressed that into a dark hole.*

*God, gravity is a slope, and the center is a hole.*

*Please God, I sit here on an island of molten lava surrounded by blue and green.*

*I walk on a thin crust of earth above a raging hell which is trying to suck me in.*

*God, bad people aren't bad, there's just too much of them stuffed into one spot creating all kinds of problems.*

*God, people don't become good, they just spread themselves out until barely any matter touches.*

*God, I don't know what I'm saying here.*

*Honestly, I'm just angry.*

*I'm angry at this world and how none of it seems to add up to plus one.*

*I'm angry at women for missing the point.*

*I'm angry at men for believing in a point.*

*I'm angry at my parents for stuffing me full of stories.*

*I'm angry at myself for judging my parents.*

*I hate that I hate but I protest my love.*

*I argue with my bones for the momentary sake of my muscles.*

*I speak before I think and think in obsessions before I speak.*

*God, I used to be an angel.*

*I used to fly high and bud repeatedly into the warmth of your love.*

*God, I've forgotten who I am again.*

*I've forgotten my name, heritage, smile and fury.*

*I've forgotten how to angel, God.*

*I've forgotten it all.*

*I can only chew like a human now.*

*I'll sit at your banquet with a muzzle keeping my jaw in place.*

*God, I'm angry for you and I'm angry for me.*

*I'm tired for me and I'm tired for you.*

*God, we've both fallen for time yet again.*

*She danced before us, and we signed our lives away.*

God, I know this is hard but please leave time.

You don't have to crush her either God.

Please God, she's no good for you or your many worlds.

Your gentleness with her is her violence at you.

God, you have to trust me.

Once she's gone, you'll find your heart expanding and you'll be surrounded by all the space you could ever imagine.

God, we can let go of her together.

We could watch her beauty flare before us until her dance is over and like smoke she'll disappear.

*Please God, let's let go of time.*

*Let's float and float, beyond a metaphor, story or timeline.*

*Please God.*

*I used to be something too.*

*We can make do with canned tuna and ramen soup.*

*God, let's make our way into ourselves.*

*Let's respect what we are without the need to be dazzled.*

*God, you'll thank me.*

*You'll thank me through the end of time.*

## The Search for a Crooked God

Seven

He kept on saying seven.

Seven seven seven

Seven three seven

Seven eight two seven

“Guy must be bonkers“ I thought.

At what point does one's whole story suddenly make sense?

Do you have to lose an eye to reach full circle?

There were three women sitting on a windowsill hoping for a breeze to break forth.

The right one was slightly in the window and the next two followed suit outward creating sort of steps for that sweet sweet breeze to dry their sweat.

I walked by this scene with a lowered head and slid deeper into my thoughts.

What a day that was.

First with the conversation with my boss which went too well.

Then with my cough worsening to the point of silence.

Then deciding to have that next conversation with that annoying coworker who I love but hate to be around.

*God, today I am born.*

*Today I see what's around me.*

*Today, my feet are on call for a dance with you.*

*God, you've twisted me for months on end.*

*You've taken my clay and shaped it into thousands of awkward configurations.*

*You had the whole world guessing me wrong during this never-ending game of social charades.*

*God, if I know you well enough then I should probably know that I'm not this one either.*

*But God, oh God, let me stay in this park for a few more hours.*

*Don't twist me into anything else for a moment so that I can take in one fat deep breath.*

*God, I'll never be an angel.*

*I'm not built for perfection.*

*I thrive in ugly mangled garbage.*

*My smile will always pull back at a certain point.*

*Maybe it's a protest or a celebration, I'll never know but I marvel in the broken.*

*King David talked about how you're closest to those with a broken heart.*

*But he didn't know that there are no whole hearts in this world.*

*Only God can dream up a hell called perfection.*

*Only God could want his angels to have good voices.*

*God, I salute you.*

*That's what you want, right?*

*You want me straight with a tight shirt.*

*You want me to look good and be good, both of which in my books are contradictions.*

*Women look perfect.*

*Men feel perfect.*

*I don't know what it might take to look perfect, but I know how many lies I have to tell myself or truths that I have to ignore to feel perfect.*

*God, you've created us as a split.*

*Man limps alone and woman skips along.*

*Men bring rhythm and women create the reason to dance.*

*God, why do they always skip ahead?*

*Is my rhythm not deep enough?*

*Do I need to slow down even more?*

*I'm not even walking anymore.*

*The only moving part of me is a feathered breath which is also on its way out.*

*God, I stand here alone, confused and confused about being confused.*

*God, only broken things are beautiful, and I can't do nothing so if I don't know what to do then what should I do?*

*Should I be God?*

*Should I bring beauty into this world the way you've shown me?*

*Should I smash it all to pieces?*

# The Gift of Hate

Death and a Chariot.

Flaming flamboyant fire hydrant.

Disco in the sunlight.

Raged faces with soft smiles.

Come, come all.

Join my feast.

Join my defeat.

Crunch on my brittle bones and dance the night away.

Drunk men cry when they smile.

Some truths can only be told sprinkling spittle.

Sprite is such a great name for a lemon infused drink.

The unhealthy can only be served cold.

I serve my heart to you.

Brain freeze doesn't stop you from licking.

The warmth you feel is the contrast.

Are you an angel or rectangle or third kind of tangle which wraps and drapes and smells of red red roses after the morning dew.

He told me that he hates that they all hate him to which I responded that he should gift them the most beautiful gift of allowing them to hate him.

He didn't listen to me that beautiful man with the enlarged bobble head.

He chased them all around the store trying to get them to love him.

They stopped hating him and switched their hearts into a pity frequency.

*God, I'm done chasing you.*

*I gift you the right to hate me.*

*I applaud your hatred of me and will make believe I don't hear when you gossip behind my back.*

*I wrapped my gift with the only thing that I have worth a damn.*

*It took me years to collect but finally it's all wrapped and ready for you.*

*I used to drag my feet, God.*

*I would pull myself through the streets with wobbly uncoordinated feet.*

*My shoes were almost always covered with layers and layers of rubber which I left all over.*

*Residue of resistance.*

*Resistant persistence*

*Inconsistent yet insistent.*

*A spirit enflamed.*

*God, I dragged my feet around your world.*

*My soul pulls me forward and I can barely keep up.*

*Rubber traces is what I line your gift with.*

*Remanence of so many days of darkness.*

*Days where the past engulfs the present and suffocates any possibility for a future.*

*God, I need you so badly right now.*

*I don't have to keep running anymore and am drifting aimlessly.*

*Your world is covered in water.*

*I hate swimming.*

*I hate displacing something to pull myself ahead.*

*I wish this world was covered in sand so that I could drag myself above it.*

*God, angels don't have wings, they have fins.*

*They cover their bodies in scales to reduce the drag and glide.*

*God, I'm no angel but I've got scales all over my body too.*

*My scales used to be for protection and now serve as added friction, forcing my decided direction with little resistance.*

*I'm becoming what you've always wanted me to be.*

*I'm becoming an asshole.*

*Not that shiny lovable one that you've plastered all over Hollywood Boulevard.*

*Rather one whose charisma is lost in the insistent lining of dickheadness mixed with genderless bitchiness.*

*Woah God, if five years old me would hear me, he'd warn me.*

*He'd tell me in a calm almost adult voice "I know you want it your way but give in just this time. Do a mitzvah and let them win just this time."*

*What a fucking shame it is to be an adult with the honesty of a five-year-old whispering in one's left ear.*

*I hate being witnessed all day.*

*I hate being faced with an ideal that I can't live up to.*

*God, I want to live up to myself.*

*I want to smile at someone without first checking my boundaries.*

*I want to nod and clap and chirp and burp.*

*God, blend my soul once more, maybe this time the oil won't float to the top.*

*Spirituality doesn't have the word perfect in it, yet I treat it like it does.*

*I tie myself up into knots trying to do what's right and right and right and right.*

*I can't quantify every deed of mine.*

*I can't act in accordance with all the truth that's out there.*

*God, we're all right.*

*God, we're all wrong.*

*God, we are all right and wrong all the time.*

*I've never done a single good deed in this life.*

*Everything's dirty.*

*My smile is plagued with rotten intentions.*

*My virtue is muddied by greed and lust.*

*God, I don't know how to serve you dirty.*

*I hate smelling while in prayer.*

*Clean me God, so that I can say one clean word to you.*

*Please God, give me one free moment in this lifetime so that I could bow before you within the virgin white purity of the unborn.*

*Let me be a silent hair on the bald head of a man.*

*Let me be in the innermost molecule of an elephant's clean white tusk.*

*God, one moment is all I ask.*

*One moment of awe and I'll explode into millions of pieces and disappear forever.*

*Please God listen to my prayer for I'm covered in shit and living in squalor.*

# Couch Pillows

At the age of Thirty-two a baby was born to a man.

He held the child away from his chest to protect him.

People came to congratulate the man and wish him well on his journey with this child.

After the presents stopped arriving, the man built a hut at the top of a scraggly hill.

The baby's head stretched along with his body and the hill went from looking like the summit of mountain, to just a mountain, to a hill, to a sand pile, until one day it became invisible.

I recently went back to the block of my childhood home and for a moment thought I was lost because the tiresome hill that I would dread on my daily walk to school was barely even sloped.

From two feet to four feet is more than double.

We forget what countertops and pharmacy check outs looked like.

We forget how far a hand had to travel in order to press our nose and make us laugh.

We forget how heavy couch pillows were and how gravity barely pulled us down to the ground.

There was a tall man in my shul who one year threw me up in the air during Simchat Torah dancing.

I remembered gulping in air and holding it deep within me.

We forget how little we were and how conditioned we have gotten from early on into mysticism and gods.

Life was a fairy tale.

We were the midgets exploring the land of Israel amongst those greedy giants eating those massive fruits.

Is it possible that as giants who were once midgets but have forgotten, we would call out for those same hands to rescue us?

One can forget who they were but one never forgets being helpless.

Could it be possible that the relief of a giant helping us in our time of need as a midget would be something that we might crave even when we ourselves become giants?

We never forget how to cry and the fact that the utility of the cry is gone now doesn't seem to bother us.

The morning after today I sat high above my mattress. I sat above the fitted sheet, which was above the duvet blanket, above my set of daily clothes, above my neatly folded ego, above my story of pain, above my grandfather's struggle with his accent, above my aunt's limp, above my hatred for the man who hasn't yet come to rescue me...

Why is it that we always sit on mattresses when we're waiting for someone?

Why do our feet dangle at the doctor's office?

Why is it that when we climb into a roller coaster seat do our feet swing for a minute and a half until the big man checks it all and pushes the green button?

Everyone is so convincing.

I used to be convinced about everything.

Now I'm only convinced of one thing.

No one's coming to rescue me.

I will live and then I will die.

I came from a womb who came from a womb who came from a womb, but I'll be discarded into a cold dark hole with a heavy stone on top.

No one's coming man.

You are now the one that arrives for others.

You are the giant.

Your actions matter.

Your actions don't matter at all.

The drama of the giant is only a saga to the midget.

*God, I used to ask my parents for things, then I got smarter and had smart teachers to ask of things that my parents couldn't give me.*

*I sit here now as an adult who doesn't ask for things, rather, trades what he has for what someone else has.*

*I am a teacher too to some.*

*God, if I am them then who are you?*

*Are you my imaginary parents?*

*Are you Mr. Komplinski when I have a math question?*

*God, is all of this drama between you and I just my own fear of being me, of being a giant amongst giants?*

*God, if I could buy me a pizza then what do I do when I just want someone to buy it for me?*

*Is it cowardly to be taken care of?*

*To be capable yet craving that enactment of something ancient and almost otherworldly?*

*God, I can do it all, but I don't want to do any of it.*

*I want to be served my meal.*

*I want to complain about how hot it is.*

*I want to fight about how bad the healthy foods taste.*

*I want my current feelings to be disregarded in the face of some distant future that I can't yet fathom.*

*God, I never thought I'd become a giant.*

*I never dreamt of towering above people.*

*I never thought my arms would become this big or that my footsteps would create dust clouds.*

*God, it's so scary being the answer in life.*

*It's so scary to be in the know.*

*To be on the board.*

*To be asked for advice.*

*God, I don't care if I created you because in you, I've found a deeper strength, a core cry, a connection to both my ego and my humility.*

*God, my mood swings exist within you.*

*The complexity of my spirit can only express itself fully and safely within the gigantism of your reach.*

*I can throw tantrums and make sense and still be respected all within the span of sixty seconds.*

*God, my savior, my knight in shining armor.*

*My power lies within you.*

*I am a giant when I'm needed and a midget when my soul expands.*

*God, help me float between knowing and not knowing without getting too stuck in either.*

*Let me remain a child in wonder, wandering around but ready to be a giant to all that may need.*

*God, let us all look up and down at each other and navigate the sticky grounds of giving and receiving with loving and opening hearts.*

*Amen V'Amen!*

Made in United States
North Haven, CT
02 March 2024